Empowering Your Pupils through Role-play

It can be hard to get children to talk about their feelings . . .

Empowering Your Pupils through Role-play reveals the power of role-play in creating a safe space for pupils to explore emotions and build resilience through performance, discussion and the sharing of ideas, whilst enabling teachers to meet curriculum outcomes.

Designed to enhance personal development, the practical activities help pupils become effective communicators and active investigators. Working independently of the teacher, pupils collaborate with their classmates to build trust, and can be actively involved in group activities, or take part as observers and commentators.

Children know and understand about values by experiencing them. Throughout this book there are opportunities for teachers to involve their pupils in:

- performing
- writing
- directing
- drawing
- designing
- building.

The activities in *Empowering Your Pupils through Role-play* are challenging and designed to move pupils towards becoming alert and responsible young adults, actively able to engage with others and equipped with the skills to develop relationships and trust. The extensive resources section contains warm-up games, tips on writing and activities for mime, movement and improvisation.

Teachers of children aged 4–11 with an interest in Pers Health Education will find this a practical and inspirational

Rosanna Morales is an experienced author and teacher.

Empowering Your Pupils through Role-play

Exploring emotions and building resilience

Rosanna Morales

Routledge
Taylor & Francis Group

LONDON AND NEW YORK

First published 2003
by Curriculum Corporation, Australia
reprinted in 2003
This edition published 2008
by Routledge
2 Park Square, Milton Park, Abingdon, Oxon OX14 4RN

Simultaneously published in the USA and Canada
by Routledge
270 Madison Ave, New York, NY 10016

Routledge is an imprint of the Taylor & Francis Group, an informa business
© 2008 Rosanna Morales

Typeset in Garamond and Helvetica by
RefineCatch Limited, Bungay, Suffolk
Printed and bound in Great Britain by
TJ International Ltd, Padstow, Cornwall

British Library Cataloguing in Publication Data
A catalogue record for this book is available from the British Library

Library of Congress Cataloging in Publication Data
Morales, Rosanna.
Empowering your pupils through role-play: exploring emotions
and building resilience / Rosanna Morales
        p. cm.
1. Role playing. 2. Affective education. 3. Emotions in children.
4. Resilience (Personality trait) in children. I. Title.
LB1072.M65 2008
370.15'3—dc22

                                                        2007021203

ISBN10: 0–415–44708–9 (pbk)
ISBN10: 0–203–93576–4 (ebk)

ISBN13: 978–0–415–44708–9 (pbk)
ISBN13: 978–0–203–93576–7 (ebk)

Illustrations by Nick Buttfield
Worksamples by Salvador Hammond

Contents

Introduction   vii

BULLYING   **1**
Research activity   2
    Bullying interview   2
Monologues   3
Role-play exercises   9
    Who is the bully?   9
    It wasn't me   11
Interactive play   13
    Miss Poetry   13
Art and writing activities   21

GRIEF   **22**
Research activity   23
    Write a letter   23
Monologues   24
Role-play exercises   29
    Now that you've gone   29
    Moving on   31
Interactive play   32
    Rachel's dog   32
Art and writing activities   36

ANGER   **37**
Research activity   38
    Angry words   38
Monologues   39
Role-play exercises   45
    I'm the hockey captain   45
    Job sharing   47

Interactive play   48

   I don't want to hear this   48

Art and writing activities   53

SELF-ESTEEM   **55**

Research activity   56

   My best points   56

Monologues   57

Role-play exercises   62

   145cm tall   62

   Julie's birthday party   63

Art and writing activities   65

RESOURCES   **68**

Creative role-play activities   69

   Ditto   69

   Statues   71

   Stop the action   73

   From the top   75

   The Village Square   77

   Setting up a role-play area   84

Warm-up starters   86

   One mouth   87

   Weird positions   88

   Mood zones   89

   Creature feature   90

   Pause   91

   Speakers and actors   93

   Blabber touch   94

   Danger switch   95

   Swift swap   96

   Pick it up   97

   BBC World News   98

   Set alive   99

   Numbers   99

Tips and hints on writing for a performance   100

   Writing a monologue   100

   Structuring an interactive play   107

   Interviewing   109

Introduction

The importance of role-play

Getting students to talk about their feelings is not always easy. There are many issues that are hard for them to talk about because they may be afraid of ridicule or dismissal. Students need to be given permission to play and explore. Role-play can help them 'play' with personal problems. It allows them to be spontaneous by releasing creative energy. By gathering together in the safe environment of the classroom to hear and share stories, all students can feel they have a place in their class, school and community.

Why use this book

This book can be used in English, Drama and Health Education classes. It has been designed to enhance personal development through performance, discussion and sharing of ideas. Students are enabled to go on imaginative journeys as they rehearse for real life. Through role-play, students can begin to take responsibility for themselves, take charge of their own actions, and experiment with various solutions to problems.

The activities in this book emphasise the creative process rather than working towards a big production. They are designed to help students become effective communicators and active investigators. In addition, students are given the opportunity to work independently of the teacher by collaborating with their classmates, thus building trust.

The activities are also designed for various learning styles. There are opportunities for drawing, writing, performing, directing, designing and building. Learners can be actively involved in the group activities, or can take part as observers and commentators.

The topics are designed to encourage students to listen and to understand what others are feeling. By writing stories and plays individually or as a group, students learn to take responsibility for their own learning. They also have the opportunity to give each other snapshots of their lives in a supportive environment and to support and accept themselves and others. The aim is to instil individual confidence and group cohesion.

The teacher's role

Teachers do not have to be experienced in drama. The role of the teacher in these activities is to let the students lead the activities but to be there as a guide. Your main role is to brief the students at the start of every activity, and allow students to volunteer for the roles. There will be times when students will not want to be actively involved. They can be observers, recorders or reviewers instead. It is also important that you are aware of students' reactions to the activities and to be ready to debrief the class. Although creative role-play can help students develop their imagination as well as help them with problem solving and interpersonal skills, it is important that this takes place in a safe environment in which students practise skills and learn from their mistakes as they *pretend*.

Getting started

This book offers a new approach that encourages students of upper primary and lower secondary year levels to act out a play or monologue and then discuss how the characters may deal with a particular issue. There are open questions at the end of the plays or monologues that focus on the topics of bullying, grief, self-esteem, anger.

---

*If you are introducing drama to your class for the first time or you have students who seem reluctant to try the activities, you can introduce the role-play topics with the **Warm-up starters** in the **Resources** section. These are indicated in the topics by: The Resources section also contains tips on the writing activities in the book.*

The **Warm-up starters** are easy and do not need props, costumes or scripts. They are simply fun activities that are more like a game than a lesson. They are intended to get students ready to work on their own improvisations.

Students need to feel safe, relaxed and, most of all, confident before taking on any of the activities. It is important that you know your students and their learning preferences. Some students may wish to focus more on the art or writing activities. Your students can also **improvise** if the language in the monologues or plays is unsuitable.

The topics

This book deals with personal and social issues – **Bullying, Grief, Anger** and **Self-esteem**. Young people face these issues on a daily basis. Some cope better than others. However, they all need guidance and support as they develop their individual strategies. There is no right or wrong way of resolving a conflict; it is matter of finding the right way for each individual without physical and psychological harm.

Each topic contains some of the following activities.

Research activities

These begin each topic and are designed to get students thinking about the topic.

Monologues

The monologues have several formats and voices. They reflect various ages and personalities. You may need to be selective in which ones your students read. There are also various ways of using these monologues in class:

☐ Divide the class into groups. Ask each group to choose one of the monologues to present to the rest of the class. This can be acted out or treated as a radio play or a book reading. Students may even want to mime the monologue with a narrator. In that way, most of the group could take part.

☐ Students could read the monologues individually and then discuss them in groups or as a class.

Team work: If a group chooses to present the monologue as a performance, students will need to choose a director, performers, costume and set providers, etc.

Lesson time: This activity can be done in a variety of ways. You may wish to give the group two to three lessons to work together on the performance pieces.

Role-play exercises

The exercises are intended to give students the opportunity to be centre stage in front of an audience of their peers. These exercises are similar to improvisation and whatever occurs in the presentation and exploration becomes a part of the scene.

There are two types of role-play exercise:

☐ Scenario with suggested conclusion. The actors are given profiles of their characters and a scenario.

☐ Scenario with performance guidelines.

Plays

There are two types of play:

☐ **Interactive plays** which include a number of alternative endings. They appear in the topics on **Bullying** and **Anger**. The students are involved in the outcome of the play by choosing from several pathways that the main character can take. A role in the play is that of Choice Host, who introduces the main character's choice with the words '**Should have said . . .?**'. Before the play can proceed, the students must discuss the questions posed as part of the play.

☐ **Scripts** are designed to be read or performed. These appear in the topics on **Grief** and **Self-esteem**. In the topic on Grief, there are two versions of a play. Students can read or perform both and then discuss the issues and the differences between the versions. In the Self-esteem topic, students are presented with a short story and a play and are asked to transform them into another genre. The first script can also be used to create role-plays.

Follow-up activities are provided at the end of each type of play to stimulate discussion in a group setting. It is also possible for students to improvise dialogue in the plays.

Teacher's note: Hand out the script (and accompanying flow chart in the case of the interactive plays). Ask for volunteers to be the actors, set designers, directors, etc. Once all the roles have been assigned, give the students time to set up the play as they wish. You may need to give them a lesson to rehearse and to work out the stage layout. If time permits, you may give them a few weeks to rehearse the play, or they can read from the script.

Flow chart: The flow chart shows the alternate pathways in the script. It clearly shows how the scenes have been structured and the points at which decisions are to be made.

Art and writing activities

Each topic concludes with some art and writing activities. There may be a comic strip for students to complete by drawing their own characters or filling in the speech bubbles. There are personal profile posters to create, as well as an observation journal to design and maintain.

Resource section

This section of the book offers a number of activities, from **creative role-play activities** to writing monologues and interactive plays to setting up a permanent role-play area in the classroom. It also has a series of **warm-up starters**, which can be used to introduce a topic or motivate students. They can also be used as fun activities in other contexts.

All the activities in the book are designed as handouts which can be photocopied. These pages are indicated by the header:

The physically interactive activities in the **creative role-play** section will help students see that they have the power to change injustices or hurts they see around them by listening, watching and planning their actions.

The activities are challenging and are designed to move students towards becoming alert to and actively engaged with others in order to develop relationships and trust.

Some of the role-play activities are based on traditional forms of theatre where dialogue is created between audience and stage.

BULLYING

No doubt bullying has affected you and your students. It is a topic that is dealt with in all schools. Unfortunately it is a continuing problem. What is important is for students to feel that they are not the only ones dealing with this issue. Young people can feel uncomfortable talking about being a victim. They are also afraid to report others. However, through taking an active or passive part in these role-play activities students can explore the alternatives available to them.

Getting started

The following research activity is a good way to start this topic. Students can do an interview outside school and then report back to the class or to a group. They may also convert the interview or conversation into a monologue which they can present themselves or alternatively have another student perform to the rest of the class. It may also be a good idea to read through one of the monologues in this chapter as a class before the students begin writing up their interview questions.

 The **Resources** section has a variety of hints on how to approach writing and also describes the value of setting up a permanent role-play area in the classroom.

Research activity

Bullying interview

Ask a friend or a family member if they have ever been affected by bullying. If they have, write out a list of questions then make an appointment to interview them. Remember that sometimes it is hard for people to talk about a bad memory so let them read the questions you are going to ask before the interview. You will need to take notes during the interview. All interviews must remain *anonymous*.

Follow-up

After your interview, write out, in point form, what the main issues were for that person. For example:

How did they feel?

How did the bullying affect them?

What did they do about the bullying?

Once you have jotted down these main points write a monologue based on the interview. You may present the monologue to the class yourself or you may choose someone else to present it for you.

Monologues

Jessica

> When I was in year 5 and year 6 a girl bullied me nearly every day. I still remember her name, how she looked and where she lived. I even remember all the terrible things she did to me in detail – even though it was nearly eight years ago.
>
> When I think of that time at primary school all I can think of is how bad I felt. How that girl took over any good memories I had of primary school. My memories are of being tripped over as I walked into our classroom, being pushed, or cruel notes being stuck on my back for all to see as I walked home from school, rumours being spread about me. Sometimes they would cover my back with chalk. And you know what? I never fought back. I didn't even try. It is the one thing I will regret forever. Maybe things could have been better and the bullying would have stopped.

Questions

How do you think Jessica explained the chalk on her clothes to her mother?

What are some of the things Jessica could have done to fight back?

Why do you think the bully kept picking on Jessica?

What about Jessica's friends? Do you think she would have had many?

Empowering Your Pupils through Role-play © Rosanna Morales, Routledge 2008

Harry

It's easy to be a bully. All you
have to do is pick a good
victim. Usually I pick kids
that are smelly, or different.
I especially like the ones that
cry easily. All I have to say
is 'Cry baby, cry baby'. It's
so funny to watch them cry
and run away to hide just like
little babies. Sometimes I bully
kids for no reason at all but
first I have to be quite sure that
they are not going to fight back.
I'm not going to let anyone bully me.

Sometimes kids stand up to me and
so I have to fight them. That's
what Dad tells me to do. He says,
'Don't let anyone push you around.
Show them who's boss.' My Dad's
pretty tough.

Questions

Which kind of person makes the best victim?

What kind of person is Harry?

What kinds of friends do you think he would have?

Empowering Your Pupils through Role-play © Rosanna Morales, Routledge 2008

6 TYPES OF BULLIES

There are all sorts of bullies. You can be pushed, threatened, yelled at and made fun of. Even bullies get bullied!

Complete the panels below...

Don't argue! Do it my way.

Always thinks he's right. Never listens to your opinion.

Mr Always Right

Miss Love Myself

Always wants what does not belong to him.

Mr Give Me

Miss Gossip

ONE WAY TO STOP BEING A VICTIM IS TO STOP THINKING LIKE ONE.

Pocket tip...

Bullies like to control others by stealing personal items.

Put your name on everything that you need to take to school. That way you can prove it is yours. Don't take anything that is important or valuable to school.

'I would like my pencil back.'

Pocket tip...

Most bullies are too afraid to repeat a remark they have made.

Ask them to repeat whatever they've said. This usually makes them feel really stupid and self-conscious.

'Say that again, please.'

Empowering Your Pupils through Role-play © Rosanna Morales, Routledge 2008

GRIEF

Grief can be caused by many events: a relative or friend dying, a school friend moving to another school, or a parent moving out due to separation. Grief can also bring up feelings of anger and guilt. This can cause a lot of confusion.

 Ditto, a creative role-play activity in the **Resources** section, is a great activity for students to act out grief. It will help the class to see where the pain is and offer ways of dealing with it.

Encourage the students to write down their feelings as often as possible. Perhaps introduce a **feelings journal** where they can enter their thoughts at the end of every day during a time of grief.

Getting started

The **family tree** outlined in the art activities section in this chapter is also a way to introduce this topic. These activities may help to deal with grief by reflecting on the lives of those that have gone.

Research activity

Write a letter

It can be very difficult to say goodbye to someone you love. Perhaps you or someone you know did not get the opportunity to say goodbye before the person died or went away.

It is important to let people know how much you love and care for them.

Write a letter to someone you love. Tell them how much you love them and how important they are to you. They can be living or dead. Love does not end with death.

OR

Write a letter to someone you miss. Most of us have a best friend at school or in our neighbourhood. Sometimes our friends have to move house or go to another school. Write to them and tell them how much you miss the times you had and how much you miss having them around. Keeping in touch is a great way to keep a friendship going, even if you don't see each other as often.

Monologues

Alex

> Sitting by myself again. I used to be Ben's best friend. I remember the first day we met at primary school. We had the same shoes on, except mine were red and Ben's were blue. We swore we would be friends forever and that we were going to play together for ever and ever.
>
> Where are you now Ben? Are you off with your gang of friends? Do you see me sitting here alone, missing you? You don't know how hard it is for me to watch you playing with other kids. I just sit here, hour after hour, day after day, watching.
>
> I'm not alone though. Sure, everyone at home loves me. I have the perfect family. At least I've got them.
>
> At our old school everything was wonderful. Ben and I played together every day. On rainy days, after school, we would sit in his dad's car and talk for hours. We would read games manuals together and swap cards. We did everything together. But during the second term at high school everything changed. I don't know why.
>
> Ben occasionally stops and talks to me. Just last week he asked me if he could borrow my ruler. I really don't want to spend my time at high school watching him from this bench. I must look so pathetic. It doesn't look like I have a choice, does it?

Questions

Why is Alex choosing to sit on her own?

Why is she missing her best friend?

What has happened to Ben?

What choice does Alex have?

Maggie

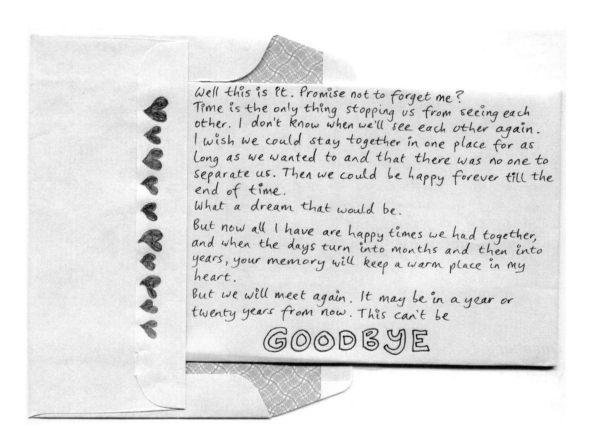

Well this is it. Promise not to forget me?
Time is the only thing stopping us from seeing each other. I don't know when we'll see each other again.
I wish we could stay together in one place for as long as we wanted to and that there was no one to separate us. Then we could be happy forever till the end of time.
What a dream that would be.

But now all I have are happy times we had together, and when the days turn into months and then into years, your memory will keep a warm place in my heart.

But we will meet again. It may be in a year or twenty years from now. This can't be

GOODBYE

Questions

Whom do you think Maggie is missing?

Do you think Maggie will be forgotten?

What should she do to keep in contact with that person?

Vince

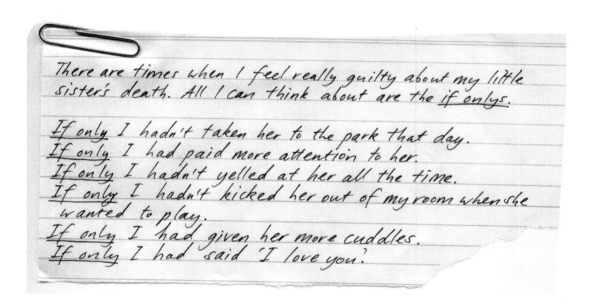

There are times when I feel really guilty about my little sister's death. All I can think about are the if onlys.

If only I hadn't taken her to the park that day.
If only I had paid more attention to her.
If only I hadn't yelled at her all the time.
If only I hadn't kicked her out of my room when she wanted to play.
If only I had given her more cuddles.
If only I had said 'I love you'.

Questions

What is Vince feeling right now?

What can he do to deal with these feelings?

Nicky

I'm sure I'm not the first person to move to a new neighbourhood or to move to a new school. But it feels like I'm the first person to move to a new life without my dad. This stinks. He has just decided to leave us. I haven't seen him for ages. He could be dead for all I know. Disappeared. Gone without a trace.

How am I supposed to feel? I know I used to drive him nuts with all my demands when we went shopping. And my continuous requests for money. But how did that make me any different to anyone else? And what about my mum? Well, she's no saint either. She was always on the phone chatting to her girlfriends.

How are we going to manage without him? We really miss him. I miss his van out the front. I keep hoping it will be there, parked at our new address, when I get home from school.

Questions

What should Nicky do to deal with her grief?

How do you think her mum feels?

How do you think her dad feels?

Empowering Your Pupils through Role-play © Rosanna Morales, Routledge 2008

Helen

> Oscar was my little brother Tri's pet dog. A car hit Oscar while we were at school. We came home and he was gone. When Mum told us Oscar was put to sleep, Tri thought Oscar would wake up soon and come back. When Mum told him that Oscar was gone forever he began to worry that if he went to sleep he might never come back either.
>
> Tri kept asking Mum all these questions: 'How did Oscar die? What did the vet do? Who took him to the vet? Did he cry? Where was he buried? Can I see him?' One by one Mum answered all his questions. Finally she said,
>
> 'Oscar won't be coming back.'

Questions

What can Mum and Helen do to help Tri deal with Oscar's death?

Tri is younger than Helen. What do you think Tri understands about death?

Role-play exercise 1

Now that you've gone

When somebody you know dies or goes away you feel sad. You miss them and feel lonely. You may also feel angry. Don't try to hide your sadness. It is important that you show your feelings openly and freely or no one will know how you are feeling and be able to help. People will be there to listen if you ask for support. Sometimes people do not know what to do or say in case they upset the person more. If we don't tell people what we need, we remain a victim, and it is difficult for victims to heal.

Getting started

To take part in this role-play exercise you need to choose one of the character profiles. Your character can be male or female and can be any age. To start the role-play, character 1 sits alone and the other three characters come in one at a time. They each sit down and talk with character 1. Eventually, they are all sitting together discussing the loss.

Scenario

A member of character 1's family has died. Character 1 needs help from the other characters to work out what they need and to let others know what they need. Character 1 thinks that the other members of the family don't care and are not around when character 1 needs them.

Character profiles

CHARACTER 1

A family member that you were very close to has died.

You feel lonely and don't know what to do to deal with your loss.

CHARACTER 2

You are related to character 1 but you have not been around because you don't know what to do or say. You are afraid that by helping you may create more pain.

CHARACTER 3

You have just found out about the death.

Your grieving has not yet begun.

CHARACTER 4

You have had a family member recently die and know that the best way to deal with your loss is to talk about it.

> ### Follow-up activity
> Make a list of three scenarios using the same profiles.
> Use the same scenario and write a new set of profiles.

Role-play exercise 2

Moving on

Getting started

Divide the stage into three zones. Each zone represents an emotion. The first zone is angry, the second zone is sad, and the third zone contains happy memories. Move from zone to zone during the course of the conversation and take on the emotion of the zone you are in.

Scenario

A new family has moved into the neighbourhood. They have recently lost a family member to a fatal disease. You must respect the privacy of the family and must not ask any personal questions about the death. Spend time to get to know them and console them if they decide to talk about their loss.

Roles

Student 1 – New family member

Student 2 – New family member

Student 3 – Person living next door on the right

Student 4 – Person living next door on the left

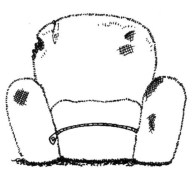

sad armchair   happy stool   angry chair

Empowering Your Pupils through Role-play © Rosanna Morales, Routledge 2008

Interactive play – Rachel's dog

Here are two versions of a play. Read them or watch them being performed by your class mates, discuss the questions, then note down the differences. *Things to look for are how Rachel and Hannah deal with the loss of their father, and how this loss has affected the sisters' relationship.*

Cast

Rachel – 12 years old

Hannah – Rachel's big sister

Penny – Hannah's friend

Rachel's dog – Version 1

Scene 1 – Street

Hannah is walking home from school with her friend Penny.

Hannah: Are you going to netball practice tonight?

Penny: Yep. What about you?

Hannah: I want to. Hopefully Mum can drive me down to the court. Sometimes she works late so I have to walk there with my little sister, Rachel, coz I can't leave her home alone.

Penny: I can ask my dad to pick you up if you like.

Hannah: OK. Thanks.

Penny: Great! We'll pick you up at 7. But you'd better be ready coz Dad hates waiting.

Hannah: That's fine. My dad was always punctual too.

(Hannah gets home and finds her sister, Rachel, in the garden looking for their dog, Tan.)

Rachel:	Tan! Tan! Come, girl. Where are you? Tan! *(Whistles)*
Hannah:	Rachel, Tan's probably in Dad's shed.
Rachel:	She's not there. I've checked.
Hannah:	We don't have time to go looking for her coz we have to get ready for netball practice.
Rachel:	I'm not going.
Hannah:	What?
Rachel:	I don't want to.
Hannah:	Come on, Rachel. You love netball.
Rachel:	I hate it.
Hannah:	Since when?
Rachel:	I'm not leaving till I find Tan.
Hannah:	Tan will be here when we get back.
Rachel:	No she won't. She'll be gone just like Dad.

<END>

Rachel's dog – Version 2

Scene 1 – Street

Hannah is walking home from school with her friend Penny.

Hannah:	Are you going to netball practice tonight?
Penny:	Yep. What about you?

Hannah:	I want to. Hopefully Mum can drive me down to the court. Sometimes she works late so I have to walk there with my little sister, Rachel, coz I can't leave her home alone.
Penny:	I can ask my dad to pick you up if you like.
Hannah:	Thanks, but I think we'll walk.
Rachel:	Tan! Tan! Come, girl. Where are you? Tan! *(Whistles)*
Hannah:	Rachel, Tan's probably in Dad's shed.
Rachel:	She's not there. I've checked.
Hannah:	Well check again. You know she is always there.
Rachel:	*(She keeps calling the dog.)*
Hannah:	Come on. Hurry up. We have to change into our uniforms and get to the court by 7. Penny will be there waiting for us.

(Rachel keeps calling the dog.)

Hannah:	Come on, Rach. Please get ready. We have to get walking or we'll be late. I should have accepted a lift from Penny's dad.
Rachel:	I wish it was our dad taking us.
Hannah:	So do I. I wish he was still here. I'm sad about what happened too.
Rachel:	I get really angry sometimes. It's not fair.
Hannah:	I know. Sometimes I feel bad about the times I used to hate him for not letting me do what I wanted to do.
Rachel:	Do you think it's our fault that he's gone?

(They hear the dog's bark.)

Hannah:	See, I told you. She's there.
Rachel:	I wish Dad was here. I miss him.
Hannah:	I miss him too. But there are lots of things that remind me of him.
Rachel:	Like Tan.
Hannah:	Yes, like our silly, funny Tan. Come on, let's go. Dad would not be happy with us running so late.

<END>

Group discussion

Why is Rachel so worried about finding Tan?

Why doesn't Rachel want to go to netball practice?

What is the connection between losing Tan and losing her dad?

What do you think Rachel should do?

How do Rachel and Hannah deal with the absence of their father?

How has this changed their relationship?

What differences did you notice between version 1 and version 2?

Follow-up activity

Tan, the dog, reminds Hannah and Rachel of when their dad was there. Write a short paragraph about things that remind you of a person or an animal that you care about.

WHEN SOMEONE DIES OR GOES AWAY...

you may keep dreaming about them.

you may want to keep phoning home to see if they have come back.

you can't concentrate on anything.

you may need to cry.

you become the class clown to hide your feelings.

MY FAMILY TREE

Design your family tree. Put the names of family members that have gone away in a square. Put the others in circles...

Mum — Dad

John — Mary — Owen — Ruby — Bill

Beth

Write a letter to someone you miss...

Dear

love

Empowering Your Pupils through Role-play © Rosanna Morales, Routledge 2008

ANGER

One of the best ways to deal with anger is to do something physical.

Getting started

 This topic focuses more on physical activities as outlined in the **Warm-up starters**. Start with the **Pick it up** activity. Ask the students to write down one 'angry' sentence or statement taken from a media report, which formed part of their research activity. Follow the guidelines for the warm-up and let students explore the language of anger.

 The **Statues** role-play activity is another way to start working on this topic. This activity invites students to apply a physical shape to anger. It also gives them the opportunity to see how anger looks to others in the class. Is it a big red shape that continues to grow? Is it a small round shape waiting to explode? Once the statues have settled, ask the students to describe what sort of anger they were depicting. Was it irritation, frustration, rage, etc?

Research activity

Angry words

Watch the news on TV tonight, or read a newspaper. Write down some of the angry words or expressions you find. Report back to class and use the questions below for discussion.

Questions

What was causing the anger? (feelings, events, other people?)

How can you explain the anger?

What else could they have done?

Follow-up activity

Read the following paragraph, then answer the questions.

AGGRESSIVE DRIVERS ON THE RISE

Drivers are taking out their frustration on each other in large numbers. What used to be just two people screaming at each other is now one person losing it and throwing bottles, eggs and anything else that can cause damage to other drivers. People are driving more aggressively now than they were five years ago. One out of three car accidents is caused by angry drivers. 'It's essential that we manage our anger as effectively as we manage our time', said Professor John White from

Why is road rage on the increase?

What do you think makes drivers angry?

What can drivers do to control their anger?

How would time management make a difference?

Monologues

Lucy

(Lucy is sitting at her desk and writing a letter to her friend Rebecca. When she finishes the letter she tears it up.)

> Dear Rebecca,
>
> I thought we were best friends. I thought I could tell you anything. I thought I could trust you. I thought you could keep a secret. But I was wrong. How dare you tell everyone that I like Adam! Did you stop to think for a minute how that would make me feel? How am I supposed to show my face at school knowing that everyone knows? I'm so angry with you. Really angry. I feel so hurt. You make me sick. I hope you have sleepless nights worrying about people's reactions to your inner most secret. I hate you Rebecca Anderson. I will never speak to you again.

Questions

Why does Lucy tear up her letter?

What do you think Rebecca would do if she got this letter?

Empowering Your Pupils through Role-play © Rosanna Morales, Routledge 2008

Lee

(Lee did not make the football team and he is annoyed with his coach. He is scribbling on a big piece of paper with a big red marker.)

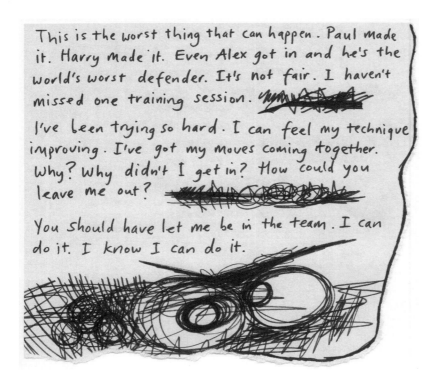

This is the worst thing that can happen. Paul made it. Harry made it. Even Alex got in and he's the world's worst defender. It's not fair. I haven't missed one training session.

I've been trying so hard. I can feel my technique improving. I've got my moves coming together. Why? Why didn't I get in? How could you leave me out?

You should have let me be in the team. I can do it. I know I can do it.

Questions

What words would you use to describe how Lee is feeling?

What can Lee do now to try and secure a place in the team next year?

Tom

> I'm forever in this room. Every time I choose to express an opinion my parents send me to my room. I mean what's wrong with standing up for my rights? Why can't I go out just because it's a school night? What's with these stupid rules? Is my social life supposed to stop between Mondays and Fridays? Well, I'm sorry but this is totally unreasonable. I can't afford to miss out on being with my friends. What would happen to my social skills? Huh? Why is a stupid Maths exam more important? Do I need to go on? Can I afford to wait till the weekend?

Questions

What do you think about Tom's parents' position?

Why is Tom so annoyed?

What compromise could Tom come up with?

Penny's mum

(Penny's mum is ringing from work. Dials the number and waits, but no answer.)

> **Where is she? She should be home by now.**
> (Dials the number again – still no answer.)

> **I'm sure she doesn't have after school activities on Tuesdays. Why isn't she home? Maybe she's at her girlfriend's place.**
> (She looks up the number and dials.)

> **Hello. This is Penny's mum. Good thanks. How are you? Is Penny there? Oh. Do you know where she might be? Well if you see her could you ask her to ring me? Thanks.**
> (Hangs up.) (Dials home again – still no answer.)

> **She's still not home.**
> (She looks up another number and dials.)

> **Hi Sally, it's me from next door. Good thanks. Have you seen Penny? Is she? Oh. I've been trying to ring her and there's no answer. Are you sure she's home? OK. Thanks.**
> (Dials the number again – still no answer but a recorded message comes on.)

> **Penny, it's Mum. Pick up the phone ... I know you're there. Please pick up the phone. Look, I'm running late again. I won't be home till late ... so ... don't wait for me to have dinner. There are some leftovers in the fridge. OK? Give me a ring and leave a message on my mobile if you need anything.**

Questions

Why do you think Penny is not answering the phone?

Do you think Penny's mum knows why she is not picking up the phone?

What should Penny do?

Empowering Your Pupils through Role-play © Rosanna Morales, Routledge 2008

Maria

Maria's family has just been told that her big brother, Joe, is very sick.

(Maria is talking to her soft toys.)

> See, I told you it was going to be bad news. Joey promised me he was going to be all right. He's getting worse and the stupid doctors can't do anything to help. They just keep saying they've done everything they can. Joey just sits there and accepts it. Even my parents have given up. How can they just accept it? We've been praying till we've turned blue in the face – and what good has that done? *(She hears a knock on the door.)*
> Go away. *(She throws one of the soft toys at the door.)* Leave me alone. *(She keeps throwing the other toys at the door.)* None of you care that Joey is dying. You've all given up. All you know how to do is pray. Well what difference has that made? Nothing! I hate you for giving up.

Questions

What would you say to Maria about being angry?

What else could she do?

Ahmed

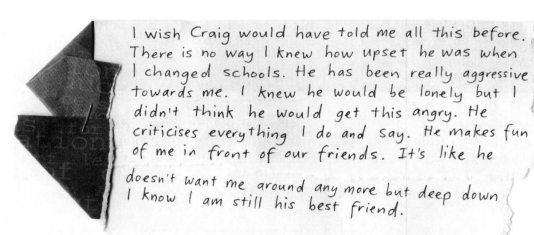

I wish Craig would have told me all this before. There is no way I knew how upset he was when I changed schools. He has been really aggressive towards me. I knew he would be lonely but I didn't think he would get this angry. He criticises everything I do and say. He makes fun of me in front of our friends. It's like he doesn't want me around any more but deep down I know I am still his best friend.

Questions

What should Craig have done instead of getting angry?

How do you think Ahmed knows that Craig is still his best friend?

Why is Craig criticising everything Ahmed does?

Role-play exercise 1

I'm the hockey captain

Anger is a very common emotion. You can learn to handle it in several ways. A good way to let your anger go is to do something physical like running, riding your bike, or even punching your pillow. Talking can also help you work through your anger. It can help you accept what is making you angry, or solve your problem in a positive way.

Getting started

To take part in this role-play exercise you need to choose one of the character profiles. Your character can be male or female and can be any age. Once the roles have been handed out, begin the role-play by setting up the room for an election meeting. Students 1 and 2, who are running for team captain, have to give a brief speech on why the others should elect them. After the speeches, students 3 and 4 can ask questions before they vote. Voting is by show of hands.

Scenario

Student 1 has been the captain of the hockey team for the last 2 years. Student 2 has just started at the school where he/she was the school sports captain. Student 1 is feeling threatened and is starting to show anger towards student 2. Students 3 and 4 are also in the hockey team and will have to choose who will be captain this year.

Character profiles

STUDENT 1

You have been captain of the hockey team for the last 2 years.

You are a good captain.

You are best friends with student 3.

STUDENT 2

You love all sports.

You would like to be a sports captain at this new school.

Your focus is on making friends first.

STUDENT 3

You are best friends with student 1.

You think student 1 is a good captain but would like to have a new one.

STUDENT 4

You are a champion goal scorer.

You are sick of student 1's tactics.

Follow-up activity

Make a list of three scenarios using the same profiles.

Use the same scenario and write a new set of profiles.

Role-play exercise 2

Job sharing

Scenario

You are at a youth group meeting. You are organising the annual camp. Various tasks are being handed out to people. Tasks include organising the tents, buying all the food, and helping the president with the newsletter. There are some people who don't want the task they have been given. However, the meeting must end with all tasks assigned.

Getting started

Start the role-play with the four people sitting at the meeting table. The youth club president can welcome everyone to the meeting and begin by giving out the tasks to the group. One by one you will respond to the task given.

Roles

Student 1 – Youth club president (also the editor of the club newsletter)

Student 2 – Happy with task of organising the tents

Student 3 – Does not want the task of organising the food; would rather work on the newsletter

Student 4 – Has been assigned to assist with the newsletter but wants the task of organising the tents

Role-play variation

The four players have a ball, which they pass to each other. They can speak only when they are holding the ball.

Interactive play – I don't want to hear this

Paul's parents are getting a divorce. He can't believe it. He always thought his parents loved each other. How is he going to explain this to his friends? He tries everything he can think of to help them change their minds. But they have decided. Paul is left feeling very angry.

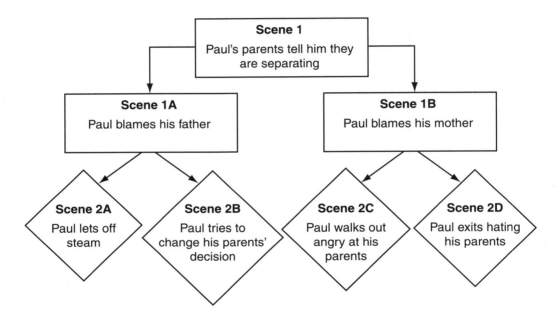

I don't want to hear this

Cast

Paul

Mum

Dad

Choice Host

Scene 1 – The kitchen

(Paul and his parents are having breakfast.)

Paul:	I don't want to hear this.
Mum:	I know this is hard for you.
Paul:	What do you know?
Dad:	It wasn't an easy decision to make.
Paul:	Well, this is the first time I've heard you mention the word 'divorce'. How long have you been discussing it?
Mum:	It's for the best.
Paul:	Who for?
Choice Host:	Should have said . . .? Here are Paul's choices:

□ *(To Dad)* It's you, right? It's your fault. It always is. (Go to 1A.)
OR
□ This can't be happening to me. (Go to 1B)

Scene 1A (Paul blames his father.)

Paul:	*(To Dad)* It's you, right? It's your fault. It always is.
Dad:	It's nobody's fault.

Empowering Your Pupils through Role-play © Rosanna Morales, Routledge 2008

Paul:	You're never home. Maybe if you were around more often this wouldn't be happening.
Mum:	Paul, please calm down.
Paul:	How am I going to tell my friends at school? It's going to be so embarrassing.
	I'm always going on about how in love my parents are. How happy we all are.
Mum:	We don't have to tell anyone now. We'll give it some time.
Paul:	Well, you've both had plenty of time to get used to the idea. What am I going to do? *(He storms off outside.)*
Choice Host:	Should have said . . .? Here are Paul's choices:

□ *(He lets off steam by bouncing his basketball around.* (Go to 2A.)

OR

□ Please tell me what's going on. (Go to 2B.)

Scene 2A (Paul lets off steam.)

Paul:	*(He lets off some steam by bouncing his basketball around.)*

<END>

Scene 2B (Paul tries to accept his parents' decision.)

Paul:	Please tell me what's going on.
Dad:	*(Dad goes to give Paul a hug.)*
Paul:	Leave me alone. I don't want to be touched.

(Dad turns to leave.)

Paul:	No, Dad. Don't go. I'll try to be better. I'll help you and Mum with the chores. I'll do my homework and reading. I'll go to bed without complaining.
Dad:	Paul, you know we both love you very much.
Mum:	We'll try and work through this together but it's going to take some time.
Paul:	But I can make it better for us, right now. I'll help you. I promise. Just ask me for anything.
Dad:	The best thing you can do is to give it some time. We all need time to think things through.

<END>

Empowering Your Pupils through Role-play © Rosanna Morales, Routledge 2008

Scene 1B (Paul blames his mother.)

Paul:	This can't be happening to me.
Mum:	It doesn't have anything to do with you, Paul.
Paul:	Can't the two of you work things out?
Dad:	We've tried. But it's not working out.
Paul:	How bad can things be?
Dad:	We both have our reasons.
Paul:	What's your excuse, Dad? Does Mum nag you too much?
Dad:	Stop, Paul. Please.
Paul:	Admit it. If she wasn't always on your back we wouldn't be having this conversation.
Choice Host:	Should have said . . .? Here are Paul's choices:

☐ I'm going to have to change schools. (Go to 2C.)

OR

☐ I can't believe you're doing this to me! (Go to 2D.)

Scene 2C (Paul walks out angry at his parents' decision.)

Paul:	I'm going to have to change schools.
Mum:	There's no need for that. You're not the only one at school whose parents are separated.
Paul:	But all my friends have parents that are still married.

(Paul walks out, angry at his parents' decision.)

<END>

Scene 2D (Paul exits, hating his parents.)

Paul:	I can't believe you're doing this to me!
Mum:	Sorry, honey, but that's the way things have turned out.
Dad:	We'll make it work out for all of us.
Paul:	*(Angrily)* Stop lying to me! I'm not a child!
Mum:	We're not lying, Paul. We will try to make things work.
Paul:	This is the worst thing that has ever happened to me. I will never forgive you for this. NEVER!
Dad:	Paul, stop.

Paul: You can make all the promises in the world. I hate both of you. You used to love each other. You used to love me. Now you don't care about any of us.

Well, don't expect me to care for you! (*Walks out.*)

<END>

Follow-up activities

Group questions

What thoughts may be going through Paul's head while he is playing around with his basketball?

What do you think made Paul so angry?

How do you feel when Paul shows his anger?

Why is Paul feeling guilty?

Compare the four endings and describe how Paul is feeling in each one.

Design the structure of a play with different endings

The flow chart above shows four different endings to the play. Use this chart to design your own play structure. You may add more endings. Use rectangles to show the scenes and diamond shapes to show the endings.

I GET ANGRY WHEN... (Draw a picture to explain why.)

Things I say when I'm annoyed.

Things I say when I'm irritated.

Things I say when I'm mad.

Get anger out of your head. Write it down, then tear it up.

_____

_____

_____

_____

_____

IT IS WRONG TO TAKE YOUR ANGER OUT ON OTHERS.

Pocket tip...

Let off steam – go for a run.

Empowering Your Pupils through Role-play © Rosanna Morales, Routledge 2008

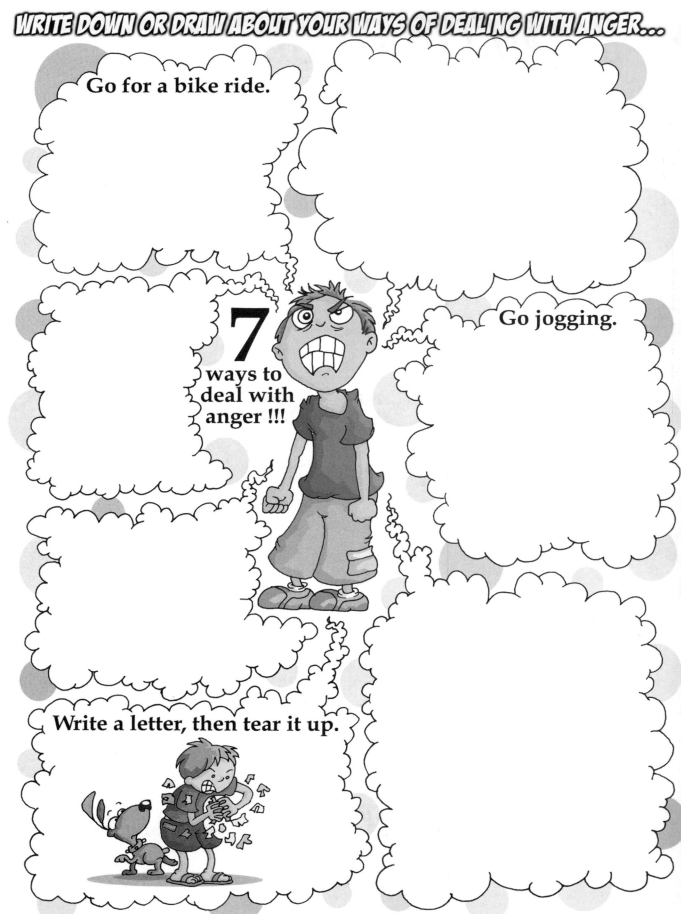

Go for a bike ride.

7 ways to deal with anger !!!

Go jogging.

Write a letter, then tear it up.

SELF-ESTEEM

Self-esteem is about how we feel about ourselves. Students should be encouraged to stop comparing themselves to others and to achieve outcomes that matter to them and that they can be proud of. The activities outlined in this chapter aim to help students focus on their strengths and encourage them not to hide their feelings of sadness, frustration or even joy.

Students bring into class issues from home, the school or the community. It is important that they know they cannot feel positive all the time, that it is OK to say 'I feel angry today because . . .' or to celebrate with the class when they are feeling good about themselves or have achieved something. It is also important for others to celebrate with them.

The **feelings slider** activity in this chapter suggests a time in the day when students can describe how they are feeling to the rest of the class. They move the slider to a point which depicts their mood; that is, how positive they are feeling today. Students can then begin to feel that there is a place and time in their daily life where they will be listened to.

Getting started

 The warm-up starter called **Speakers and actors** can be used to show how physical appearance does not always reflect inner feelings.

Research activity

My best points

1   On a sheet of paper write down as many words as you can to describe yourself.

2   Put them in two columns. The words you like most about yourself and the words you dislike about yourself.

3   Now break up into small groups.

4   Focus on one member of the group at a time. Everyone in the group tells that person a positive thing they can think of about them. One of the group members lists these.

5   Each member of the group is given their list.

6   Now compare what you have written in your two columns with the list from your group.

7   Write down what you discovered in your personal journal.

Monologues

Natalie

Everyone feels sorry for Sandy. I mean, why exactly?

Stop, don't tell me. I want to examine this for myself. Let's think about Sandy for a minute.

First of all she's a cross between a Barbie doll and Kylie Minogue. Every time I see her, I can almost hear a catwalk commentary that goes something like this:

'... and here is Sandy, ladies and gentlemen. She has captured hearts with her beauty and unique talent for making everyone and anyone do her homework for her. As you can see, today Sandy is covered in a sea of make-up with great attention to detail given to her Barbie doll look-alike blonde hairstyle. Sandy also comes with a second outfit which has been specially designed to steal boyfriends.'

Oh, dear. Maybe I shouldn't be judging a book by its cover, but, please, what's with all the layers of make-up. Has she got something to hide?

I mean, why should I feel sorry for someone who steals boyfriends and is only concerned about her looks. Does someone expect me to get through that sea of make-up and get to know her?

I mean what on earth would she get out of having *me* as a friend?

Questions

Why does Natalie think people feel sorry for Sandy?

What is Natalie's opinion of herself?

How does Natalie feel about someone looking like a Barbie doll?

What might Sandy be hiding behind her make-up? (Sandy's monologue follows.)

Sandy

> Wearing the same clothes everyday is just not on, especially to school. I wear the same clothes to school, on weekends, and for going out and stuff. In winter I wear a different set but I probably won't fit into those once I get to Year 7.
>
> No one at school pays attention to me. There's Heidi, she's kind of cool but only pays attention to me when no one else is around. She just feels sorry for me. Like everyone else at school.
>
> 'Poor Sandy'. That's what they are all thinking. I can see it. I know it. I wish I went to a school that had a uniform. At least I would look like everyone else and not stand out so much.

Questions

Why do you think we place so much importance on what we wear?

Would Sandy feel differently if her parents had more money? Why?

Would wearing a uniform make a difference to Sandy's self-esteem?

Empowering Your Pupils through Role-play © Rosanna Morales, Routledge 2008

Fran

> *Dear diary,*
>
> *This is my first entry. I'm going to tell you a little about me. All my life I have needed a way to talk to people about my feelings. People don't really know what's going on in my life, so they don't realise that what they say to you is going to hurt. Then I go home and shut myself up in my room. No one knows what it's like. Well, that's all for today.*

Questions

What could Fran do to start talking to others about herself?

What could you do to make Fran come out of her shell?

How does a diary help someone to cope with problems?

Kate

Today was pretty boring just like any other day. Angelo was boring, Rhonda was boring and Steve was boring as usual. Rhonda talked about Steve all day. I think she is going to drive me mad but that's ok. What are friends for? Right? I think he is ugly but you know that. **I LOVE ANGELO**

Umm, I am really bored right now. It was funny today at lunchtime. I pulled Jackie's chair out from under her. Me and Steve died laughing. In Art we made these stupid things out of paper mache and Science was really boring. We took a bunch of notes and watched a movie and me and Steve cracked up through the whole class coz we act really stupid in that class. Italian was boring as usual but I learned some new words today like "baciami" which means kiss me, and "amami" means love me and "abbracciami" means embrace me, or something like that. I think I'll give Angelo a call now and see if he wants to do something boring.

Questions

Why do you think Kate is bored?

Have you ever felt bored? What do you do about it?

What do you think Kate could do to change her attitude?

Empowering Your Pupils through Role-play © Rosanna Morales, Routledge 2008

John

> I didn't think I could ever do it. It wasn't an easy decision to make. But I did it.
>
> I put my name down for the student representative council. Yes, me! I could be on the SRC. Me, John Smith. The guy with the 'daggy' name. The guy with no future. The guy with no style.
>
> VOTE ① - John Smith
>
> Vote for me. Vote for a hard worker.

Questions

What do you think may have helped John to decide to run for the SRC?

What do you think John might have said other times he looked in the mirror?

Empowering Your Pupils through Role-play © Rosanna Morales, Routledge 2008

Role-play exercise 1

145cm tall

John loves to play basketball. He dreams of playing in centre position. Most of his team-mates are better players than he is. He's hopeless at shooting, he can't score enough to be a scorer, he's not so great at passing the ball and he's pretty poor on defence. He's what most people would call 'pathetic'. The fact that he is the shortest in his year makes getting the ball into the basket almost impossible.

John spends most of his time on the bench. This doesn't really bother him too much because deep down he knows it will not be forever. His best friend, Rob, nicknamed Tarzan because of his animal behaviour on the court, has been teaching him how to play a good game. John knows he is getting better. So, is this the year he will get his act together? Maybe, maybe not.

Why, you may ask, does he keep playing a game better suited to tall people? Well, it's because he loves it. It makes him feel tall. Even though most of the team are really tall they let him play just because he is so enthusiastic.

He may feel a little insignificant at times because of his height. Sure, it can be pretty frustrating being a runt and a magnet for *short jokes,* but he does know that it's not as bad as being on the receiving end of racist comments or abuse.

Follow-up activities

Read the paragraphs above then write down or discuss your thoughts on the following questions:

- ☐ **What are John's feelings about himself? Positive or negative?**
- ☐ **Why does John keep playing basketball even though he is not great at it?**
- ☐ **What should John keep focusing on to keep up his self-esteem?**

Write a short play based on **145cm tall**.

OR

Write a role-play using the paragraphs as a scenario.

Empowering Your Pupils through Role-play © Rosanna Morales, Routledge 2008

Role-play exercise 2

Julie's birthday party

Angela is a rather sensitive girl. She spends a lot of time by herself writing her private thoughts into her diary. Most people think she is a loner but the truth is she is very shy and a little self-conscious. She has a disability called *spina bifida*, which means she needs a wheelchair to get around. She's going to Julie's birthday party.

Julie's friends are arriving and handing over birthday presents as they walk through the door.

Julie: Hi, Janet. Thanks for coming. Come in.

Hi, Fran. Hi, Georgia. Hi, Pippa. This is great, everyone is coming.

(Julie closes the door.)

I can't wait to open all these presents. Go upstairs and get yourself a drink on the balcony.

(Angela knocks on the door.)

Julie: *(Opens the door. She is surprised to see Angela.)* Hi, Angela. I didn't think you would come.

Angela: I did reply to your invitation. Did you get it?

Julie: Yeah, I did, but I didn't think you were going to show up. Well come in.

Angela: Thanks.

(Angela soon realises that everyone is upstairs. She feels a little awkward and waits patiently for Julie to notice that she is on her own. In the meantime two other girls arrive at the party. They say hello to Angela and Julie.)

Girl 1:   Hi, Angela. I didn't think you were coming today?

Girl 2:   Yeah, neither did I.

Girl 1:   Julie said you weren't coming.

Julie:	No I didn't.
Girl 1:	Yes you did. You said she wasn't coming coz of the wheelchair and everything.
Julie:	*(Looking embarrassed)* Well, she obviously changed her mind. And here she is. Let's all go upstairs.
Angela:	I can't get up there with my wheelchair. Can I get up there another way?
Julie:	No *(Sarcastically)*. Great, now I have to move everything downstairs.
Girl 2:	Maybe you can ask your dad to carry Angela upstairs.
Angela:	No, that's OK. I'll stay here.
Girl 1:	But everyone is upstairs.
Julie:	*(Annoyed)* Oh this is typical. That stupid wheelchair will hog all the attention as usual.
Girl 2:	Come on, Julie. We can help you bring everything downstairs. No one will mind.
Julie:	Thanks for coming, Angela. Hope you enjoy *your* party.

Follow-up activities

Read the short play then write or discuss your thoughts on the following questions:

- ☐ **Describe how Angela is feeling?**
- ☐ **Why is Julie annoyed with Angela's wheelchair?**
- ☐ **How might a disability affect your self-esteem?**

Write a short story based on **Julie's birthday party**.

Write Angela's diary entry before and after the party.

Empowering Your Pupils through Role-play © Rosanna Morales, Routledge 2008

6 THINGS I SHOULD BE TELLING MYSELF.

When...

late at night after losing a game.	What's wrong? / Nothing. / I can't sleep. / I messed up the game. / I'll just keep trying till I get it right! / Stop thinking about it. / Why not? / You tried your best.

someone tells you they don't like you.

you wear the wrong thing.

you are under performing.

you didn't win.

you've been discriminated against.

The feelings slider

How positive do you feel today?

1. Cut out the ruler and the slider

2. Place the ruler through the slider

3. Move the slider to the position which best describes how you are feeling today.

Do this every day.

By using the feelings slider every day you can look and think about why you are feeling 100% or 70% or even 30% positive.

There is nothing wrong with sliding all the way to 10% or less.

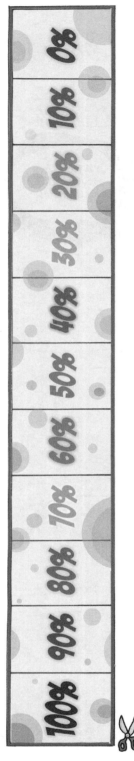

0% 10% 20% 30% 40% 50% 60% 70% 80% 90% 100%

FEELING

MOVE THIS SLIDER TO TODAY'S FEELING

50% or less days are a good time to tell the class why you are feeling low.

Talking through negative feelings can help you slide back to feeling positive.

Empowering Your Pupils through Role-play © Rosanna Morales, Routledge 2008

I AM WHAT I THINK I CAN BE!

MY THUMBPRINT

Hey! That was great!

Yeah! I knew I could do it.

Write about how you are feeling... Use all the adjectives

Dear Diary,

- pleased
- excellent
- warm
- beautiful
- thrilling
- blissful
- content
- blessed
- great
- proud
- strong

10 ADJECTIVES THAT DESCRIBE WHO I AM
Write them down then tick your favourites.

Practise signing your autograph.
Be ready for that day of fame!

COLLAGE

Cut out pictures or word phrases from magazines that represent who you are. Stick the pictures onto a large sheet of paper to create your personal collage.

What you need:

A3 sheet of paper   magazines
scissors   glue

Pocket tip...
Celebrate your achievements no matter how small.

●POSITIVE TALK   ●NEGATIVE TALK

FILL IN THE CAPTIONS

RESOURCES

Creative role-play activities

Ditto
Statues
Stop the action
From the top
The Village Square
Setting up a role-play area

Warm-up starters

One mouth
Weird positions
Mood zones
Creature feature
Pause
Speakers and actors
Blabber touch
Danger switch
Swift swap
Pick it up
BBC World News
Set alive
Numbers

Tips and hints on writing for a performance

Writing a monologue
    The story ball
    Sparkers
    What's going on?
    Brainstorming
Structuring an interactive play
Interviewing

Ditto

Notes to teachers

This role-play activity introduces an interesting relationship and collaboration between members of a group or class. A great whole-group experience, it will facilitate communication and understanding among the group. By listening to each other's personal stories, students will see that most experiences are universal. The activity also enables students to get to know members of their class and to feel they are an important part of their school and community.

Ditto can be used to deal with issues concerning the class or the school as a whole. It is a useful activity to welcome or say farewell to a class member.

Classroom layout

Setting up for this activity is very simple and requires only chairs, boxes and basic props.

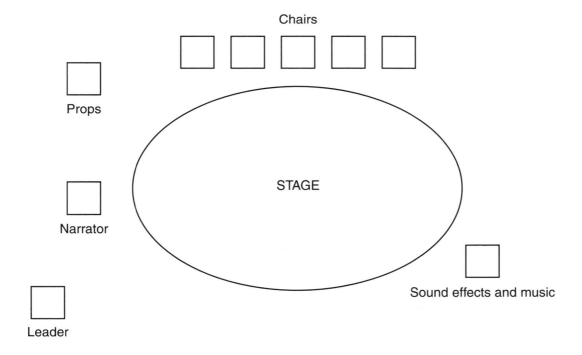

Ditto

How to

1   An audience member volunteers to be the Narrator.

2   The Narrator (or the teacher or a leader) chooses the actors to play the roles.

3   The Narrator tells a story.

4   When the Narrator has finished the story, the audience shouts 'DITTO!'.

5   The performers prepare the stage and perform the story.

6   When the performers have finished their presentation, the Leader will ask the Narrator and the audience for any suggestions and whether they think the performance offered good advice.

Try it this way

☐   The performance can take part in the setting of the Narrator's story. For example, if the story takes place on a hockey pitch, the whole group can go to the pitch to experience the performance in its original setting.

☐   Instead of acting out the story, try using movement and sound effects to create a mood that describes the emotions of the characters in the Narrator's story.

Statues

Notes to teachers

Students use their bodies to represent feelings, ideas and situations. By creating statues using different body positions, you can project your impression of a situation or feeling.

Audience members can interact by rearranging the shape of the statue, or giving suggestions, to improvise new solutions to the problems being presented.

This activity looks at body language. It can be extended into a discussion about image and how the media take different approaches to delivering information.

Classroom layout

This activity works best in an empty space. You may wish to use lights and coloured filters to create different lighting effects on the statues you create. Colour is a great way to create mood. Soft material to drape over your statues can also create a number of effects.

Statues

How to

A week before your class, choose a partner and collect newspaper articles and photos that describe people in situations where they are frightened, angry, etc.

In class

1   Use your body to demonstrate a body position that reflects your impression of the article or photo.

2   Once you are in position, your partner will read a section of the article that your statue is demonstrating to the class.

3   Select another article and then swap roles with your partner.

Try it this way

☐   You can use more than one person to create a statue. Select a story, article or photo. Then, using as many people as you need, create statues that reflect your impression of the event in the article or photo. Once you have finished, read out the article.

☐   A person reads out an article or story and everyone in the classroom uses their own bodies to demonstrate the situation or feeling in the story.

☐   As a student reads out a story, a group of five people create a statue.

☐   Audience members may rearrange statues to demonstrate a new solution to the problem.

☐   Find articles from different newspapers and magazines reporting the same story. Create statues to show how the same story can be presented in different ways to give specific impressions of what is going on.

Stop the action

Notes to teachers

A problem needs to be solved. It may or may not have a solution. There are many times when we all wish we could ask ten people what they would do to help us with a problem. Unfortunately, sometimes there is no one around or you might just find yourself in the wrong place at the wrong time. What should you do?

Wouldn't it be great if you could stop the clock and ask for advice? Or come up with that comeback line there and then rather than five minutes later. Let's role-play and build up some action plans with **Stop the action.**

The class is divided into groups. Each group works on an improvisation of the problem. This should be a short scene. Students can use dialogue or mime. The whole scene is performed. A performer then tells the audience that they will do the scene again, but that if someone in the audience wants to make a change he/she can call out 'Stop the action' and give their ideas. Other members of the audience can offer different solutions during the performance, stopping the action as required.

Through this participation, audience members can be empowered to imagine how they would deal with the situation and to practise it in a safe environment.

Classroom layout

This activity can be simple or complex. You can have a full stage set or you can just use chairs and minimum props.

Stop the action

How to

1   Make a list of issues that are affecting your friends, class, school or community.

2   Select one issue.

3   Let the audience know that they are welcome to stop the scene at any time if they think they have a suggestion to help the victim get out of trouble. Let them know that they need to shout '**Stop the action!**' Invite them up to show how the action could be changed.

4   Start your improvisation by working towards a solution.

5   If an audience member stops the action and gives a suggestion, the performer who is playing the victim needs to stand back and let the audience member show them what to do. You then need to act it out and see if that makes a difference

Audience members can continue to **Stop the action** until an agreed solution is reached.

Try it this way

☐   Act out the whole play to the end and then invite the audience to call out '**Stop the action!**' the second time you perform it.

☐   You may be having an issue that is causing concern in the whole school. Invite other classes to be in the audience.

From the top

Notes to teachers

This activity focuses on injustice or unfairness. In the activity, students present a difficulty or problem they are having in dealing with a friend or other student. They choose a class member to play the friend, tell them what they need to say and do, and act out the problem.

Most of us have had an argument or disagreement with someone. Sometimes we can argue forever and never come to an agreement. So we have to agree to disagree. Even though we may not accept someone else's belief or opinion we need to respect their right to hold that opinion. There are different ways of seeing and different ways of being.

However, there may be times when you feel unjustly treated. When an injustice has taken place most people feel the need to put it right. They need to confront the person or people by meeting with them. The need for justice can even go as far as taking a case to court, where a judge will decide if it was a case of injustice and may award compensation.

The audience watches and is then asked to comment on what the problem may be from the clues in the student's body language, and from the way they deal with the problem. The audience can then make suggestions on how a different outcome can be achieved. A second student can take the place of the student with the difficulty, which will give the original student the opportunity to see how the scenario can be changed for a better outcome.

Classroom layout

This activity can be done at the front of the classroom. Students can sit at their tables.

From the top

How to

1 A student in your class may share a story of injustice by demonstrating it to the whole class. It may be their personal story or one that has happened to someone else.

2 The student selects a class member to help demonstrate the story. She/he goes through the story and tells the helper what to do and say.

3 The injustice is re-enacted to the class.

4 The class is now invited to give advice on what should be done. Another volunteer takes the place of the student who is sharing the story to show how it could be handled differently, or what the next step should be in order to receive justice.

5 Repeat steps 3 and 4 to compare the difference. Look for differences in body language and dialogue.

Try it like this

☐ Go through the above activity steps 1 to 3.

☐ The class breaks up into groups of four to help work out a solution. They then select two of their group members to present it to the rest of the class.

☐ Compare all the presentations, select the best approach and discuss why it's the best.

The Village Square

Notes to teachers

This activity focuses on the basic skills needed to get along with others, including communication skills, how to walk away from a conflict, how to compromise, how to deal with anger and negative thoughts, and how to solve problems.

A square is divided up into smaller squares. The more squares, the longer the activity will take. Nine squares is a good number for a whole-class activity. The focus of the game can be on any theme, e.g. bullying or anger.

The students participating in the game take different parts. Two students are the players, who move around the board. They are called the Village Players. Other players are board pieces, and they are called the Village People. The rest of the students are the Village Friends, and they form the audience to offer help when required.

At the end of the game, each Village Player, with the help of the audience and the Village People, discusses the experience of the game. The teacher makes notes at each confrontation within the game, so that at the discussion stage the group can find better ways of dealing with the issues. Each playing of the game should be a learning process that helps all students to improve how they deal with problems. Storytelling is a form of ritual that produces narratives of healing, restoration and re-growth.

Photocopy as many of the profile cards as are needed. Students can also devise different character profile cards. The Village Players will need time to think about their roles.

The Village Square

The **Village Square,** like any other place, has good and bad **Village People.** How the **Village Players** deal with them depends on their communication and strategy skills. They can do it alone or with the help of the **Village Friends** (sitting in the audience). Winning the game is about the strategies you use rather than getting to the end. The **Village Judge** will decide who the real winner is.

Classroom layout

How to play the game

1   Use chalk or masking tape to create a large square and divide it into 9 equal squares. The squares must be numbered.
2   Village People stand in the squares. No more than 6. This will leave 3 squares free.
3   Village People pull a character profile out of a hat. They must act like the profile they have been given.
4   Each Village Player pulls 2 tokens out of the hat before starting the game. They can use the tokens only once.

5   Village Players roll a die, move to the square with the same number, and deal with the situation presented by the character in that square. The Village Player cannot roll the die again until the Village Judge receives the go ahead from the Village Friends.

6   The first Village Player to get to the end is the winner. But is he? The Village Judge will decide.

What you need: a die, 6 profile cards, 2 tokens per Village Player.

Each token gives a Village Player an option

☐   Avoid a conflict (use this to avoid dealing with an awkward situation)

☐   Pass on (use this to force the next Village Player to deal with this confrontation; however, you need to go back 2 places)

☐   Swap (use this token to ask the Village People to move to a different square)

☐   Village Friends (ask the Village Friends for help)

Players

Up to 6 Village People
Village Players
Village Friends (audience)
Village Judge

Try it this way

The Village Judge can sit in one of the village squares. If a Village Player lands on the Village Judge's square, a court case will take place. The Village Player will be accused of a crime and the Village Friends will act as the jury. The Village Player can choose any of the Village People to act as a witness and as a lawyer in his/her defence.

Profile cards

Bully

Bullies like to show off and make others feel small by making themselves look big and important.

Things they might do:
- Boss people around.
- Embarrass people.
- Make them feel self-conscious.
- Judge them unfairly.
- Pass blame.
- Make others cry.

Things they might say:
- Get down and kiss my shoes.
- You've got no right coming to this school.
- We can't have people like you at this club.
- Bring me some money tomorrow or else.
- You'll never get anywhere. You're an idiot.

Debater

Debaters love to argue. They will never agree with anyone and don't care if they change their mind at any time.
Debaters love to hear the sound of their own voice. They will go on and on and on.

Things they might do:
- Not listen to other opinions.
- Put people down.
- Make them feel stupid.
- Always have to have the last word.

Things they might say:
- That's ridiculous.
- I disagree with what you are saying.
- Listen to me.
- How can you think that?
- My research shows that …

Emotional

Emotional people usually react to things in rather dramatic ways. They can be self-centred and forget how their behaviour can affect others. They always forget to think before they act.

Things they might do:
- Cry at the drop of a hat.
- Get angry for no apparent reason.
- Lose their temper easily.

Things they might say:
- What about how I feel?
- You never listen to me.
- I won't talk to you ever again.
- Get out of here.

Helper

Helpers are always on the go. They will always try to help others and to make things right. They always think of practical solutions to problems. They are very generous with their time.

Things they might do:
- Take people to places they need to go.
- Fix things.
- Stop physical fights.
- Rescue people.
- Give advice.

Things they might say:
- Can I give you a hand?
- Can I fix that for you?
- I'll help you out.
- I think you had better not try that.

Avoider

Avoiders hate getting involved in anything. They usually never help out or give advice, not even when it's asked for.

They hate being the centre of attention and you will always find them at the back of any crowd.

Things they might do:

- Walk past people in distress.
- Ignore calls for help.
- Refuse to join in.
- Dislike making decisions.
- Avoid taking responsibility.

Things they might say:

- Nothing. Avoiders will do anything to get out of everything.

Setting up a role-play area

Notes to teachers

Your school may not have facilities that will enable you to put these suggestions into practice. You can improvise, however.

A role-play area is a useful area to set up in your classroom. It will remind your students that in your class that there is opportunity to play and pretend. It gives them permission to explore and practise their social interaction skills. It should always be accessible and not necessarily something you open up as a reward or for a 'drama' lesson. The props can be used to set up contexts for all subject areas.

Here is a list of suggested items you can start with. The role-play area can be built up over time.

Set items

- ☐ **Portable wardrobe on wheels** – This will hold clothing items: jackets, scarves, hats, belts and pieces of fabric of various colours.

- ☐ **Stools** – Even though you could use the normal class chairs, stools set up the expectation of a different approach.

- ☐ **Wooden boxes** – These can be used as tables, chairs or pedestals.

- ☐ **A large piece of black fabric** – This can be used as a table cloth or to hang up as a backdrop. It will cover up any regular classroom items that may be distracting. It can also form a makeshift changing room.

Prop box items

☐ **Large pieces of fabric** – These can be used as wraparounds, table cloths or flags.

☐ **Cork or lino squares** – These can create a stage area or a chessboard effect for games such as **Village Square**.

☐ **Artificial flowers** – These can be used in a variety of ways as set decoration and in various scenarios.

☐ **A large mirror** – This can be used for rehearsing monologues or to practise facial expressions.

☐ **A torch** – This can be used as a spotlight or to create special effects.

☐ **A variety of puppets** – These can be used as a teaching tool or for shy students who prefer not to speak or act out.

☐ **A variety of accessories** – Berets, beanies, little hats, floppy hats, rings and necklaces, bags and sunglasses can instantly create different characters.

☐ **CD player and CDs** with music from around the world as well as popular and classical music.

☐ **Musical instruments** – These can be hand-made or simple instruments such as cymbals, triangles and castanets.

☐ **Telephones** – Many stories can be told through telephone conversations.

Warm-up starters

Notes to teachers

This section contains a series of warm-up and group-work activities. They have been designed to get the class working collaboratively in exploring the power of physical and verbal actions and also to build students' non-verbal communication skills. The activities can be copied as handouts or explained to the class.

There are several sections in each of the handout activities.

Rules: The rules of the activity. Depending on the size of your group you may wish to add more players.

Blocking: The physical layout of the activity where relevant.

Script ideas: A situation, character or just a sentence to start off the activity.

Hints: Guidance on how the activity can be made more challenging or varied.

Try it this way: A list of alternative modes of presentation.

One mouth – whole class

Rules

The students huddle or sit very close together in a circle.

They must all speak at the same time.

No one student should lead. They must all 'speak in one voice'.

The key is to keep eye contact with other students.

Blocking

Script ideas

The whole class is an expert on junk food. An interviewer asks them about why people are addicted to it.

The whole class thinks it is God. Answer some of the following questions sent to you in the mail from a little child.

☐ *Dear God, what do you look like?*

☐ *Dear God, will you send me your reply in the mail?*

☐ *Are there any questions you would like to ask God?*

Hints

Start this activity by reciting a poem or song that the whole class knows, then move to coming up with the solution to a problem.

It is important to keep eye contact so that everyone keeps in tune with what is being said.

One player after another should take the lead.

Try it this way

One person is the interviewer and the rest of the class has to reply together in one voice.

Weird positions – 4 players

Rules

Four players take up a central position.

A situation is selected, e.g. a party.

They get into four different positions. One player must be lying down, another player standing, and so on.

Players can change position as often as they like.

If two players are in the same position, the audience must let them know.

Blocking

Script ideas

An announcement at a train station informs the commuters that their regular train has been held up due to a transport strike.

The traffic signals have stopped working at a busy junction. It is taking a long time for the traffic police to arrive.

A tin of paint has fallen from the fourth floor and landed onto a stage set up for an important speech to be delivered by the mayor.

Hints

Introduce the scene to the audience.

Try to create your own story.

Try to explain why you changed position.

Try not to hurt yourself.

Change position often, but give reasons.

Mood zones – 3 players

Rules
Divide the stage into three zones. Each zone represents an emotion. For example, the first zone can be angry, the second zone can be sad and the third zone can be happy.

Players move about on the stage and take on the emotion of the zone they are in.

They improvise dialogue or mime to match the zone.

Blocking

sad armchair   happy stool   angry chair

Script ideas
A group of three people have just received their exam results. Only one of them passed.

Three people are on a bus and one of you realises your money has been stolen. Who took it?

You have been grounded for something your brother did. Will you break your silence and tell your parents the truth?

Hints
It is important that the players use the whole stage to explore each of the emotion zones. Try to change from one emotion to the other as soon as you move into the new zone.

Try it this way
Add extra zones.

Instead of zones use furniture and props for each of the emotions.

Instead of emotions try changing your age, sex or language, or all three!

Get the audience to guess what mood you are acting out.

Creature feature – 6 players

Rules

Each player takes on the characteristics of an animal chosen by the audience.

The player must not act like an animal but must act like a person with the characteristics of that animal.

Script ideas

Your parents surprise you with something you have been wanting for a long time. However, it's not the cool thing to have any more. If only they had got you that really cool thing everyone else has at the moment.

You and your family have just moved to a new suburb. You have just joined your local sports club. You go for your first training session and no one throws you the ball. You feel left out. What do you tell your mum?

Hints

Don't make your animal characteristics too obvious. For example, if you have a cat's personality, rather than meowing, play with an object or your food like a cat plays with its prey.

Try it this way

Try acting like a household object, such as a kettle on the boil or a lawn mower that keeps cutting out.

Put the names of animals or objects on cards and the players pick them from a hat or box. The audience then has to guess which animal or object is being represented.

Pause – 6 players

Rules

This activity is made up of a series of different scenes. The first scene has one player, the next has two players, and so on.

At a point during the first scene an assigned audience member calls out **'Pause'**.

The second player moves onto the stage and starts a new scene with a completely different story.

This continues until all six players are in the scene, which they must then bring to a conclusion.

Blocking

Script ideas

Use the following lines for each player's entrance:

Player 1: This player is acting the first scene and Player 2 comes on.
Player 2: Why don't you treat me like a human being?
Player 3: Hey . . . I just remembered this dream I had last night.
Player 4: Hey, don't give me that look.
Player 5: Sorry about that, now what was I saying?
Player 6: I don't know. Maybe it was my fault.

Hints

The player or players already in the scene cannot change their position once an audience member has called out '**Pause**'. You can only change your position during a scene.

When each player enters the scene they need to find a position on stage before they start a new scene. They may wish to bring in a prop with them.

Try it this way

Each player that enters and starts a new scene brings in a prop that becomes the centre of attention.

Try it backwards. Start with six players and end with one.

Speakers and actors – 4 players

Rules
Two of the players, called the speakers, are unable to move.

They need two other players, called the actors, to act out the scene.

The speakers talk to each other and the actors act out the speech.

Blocking

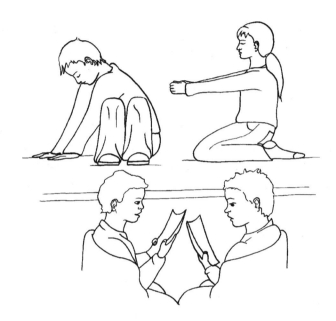

Script ideas
Discuss how important it is not to compare yourself to others.

Tell each other of your achievements and the good things about yourselves.

Hints
Before starting this activity, think of the setting in which this scene will take place. Each speaker needs to pair up with their actor so that the audience knows who is who.

Try it this way
Swap the roles so that the actors start with the motions and the speakers need to match the motions with dialogue.

Blabber touch – 6 players

Rules

Players are allowed to speak only while they are touching someone.

You are not allowed to touch someone for longer than 5 seconds.

Blocking

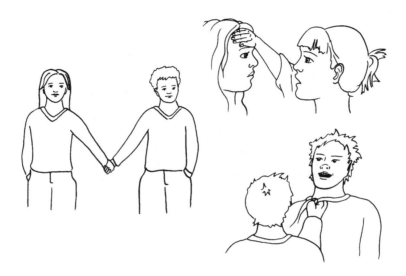

Script ideas

A group of people are at a restaurant. Each person dislikes some type of food on the menu. They all order their meal but keep changing their minds every time the waiter goes through the ingredients. They start changing the recipes, which eventually frustrates the waiter.
Each player must choose two food ingredients they dislike.

Hints

You must have a reason to touch someone. For example:
You may be meeting someone for the first time so you shake hands.
You put your hand on someone's forehead to check their temperature.

Try it this way

Players have to keep talking until someone touches them.

Danger switch – 4 players (2 players and 2 danger partners)

> ### Rules
> Players must have a danger partner who will take their place any time a scene gets too 'dangerous'.
>
> If the player needs their danger partner to help, they must call out **'Switch'**.
>
> ### Script ideas
> A boy and a girl are in the stage 'ring'. The boy has been falsely told by his friend that the girl likes him, but in fact it's the girl's best friend that really likes him. How do they tell each other the truth without hurting each other's feelings? Is this a job for danger partners?
>
> ### Hints
> Call in your danger partner when you are too scared to continue with the scene. There can be times when both danger partners are carrying on the scene. The players can re-enter the scene when they feel safe to keep going.
>
> ### Try it this way
> Each time the player calls for a danger partner, the danger partner gets weaker.

Swift swap – 6 players

Rules
Each player is given a card with a personality.

All players then stand in a circle and act out that personality.

If an audience member calls out **'Swap'**, each player must swap personalities with the player on their right, then move to a different position in the circle. The scene continues until **'Swap'** is called out again, and so on.

Blocking
All players stand in a circle.

Script ideas
Before starting the game each player is assigned a personality. One of the players has to convince the others that he/she has seen a UFO.

Every time the audience calls out **'Swap'**, the next person has to do the convincing.

Remember to swap personalities with the person on your right.

Hints
Get to know the personality of the person next to you so that you can change personality quickly when someone calls out **'Swap'**.

Start with these personalities:

☐   *an old man who doesn't believe in UFOs*

☐   *a woman who doesn't speak English*

☐   *a scientist*

☐   *a man who has been abducted several times by aliens*

☐   *a person who has to do the convincing.*

Try it this way
Have a dead character as one of the personalities.

Swap sexes.

Pick it up – 6 players

Rules

The class selects a scenario or problem to act out.

The class writes sentences on pieces of paper.

When the audience calls out **'Pick it up'**, players must stop and pick up a piece of paper with a sentence written on it.

The sentence must be included in the scene as if it was part of the script.

The player who picks up the sentence must say it immediately and the action needs to keep going.

All pieces of paper need to be picked up and used in the scene.

Try it this way

Sentences in other languages.

Drawings.

Blank pieces of paper.

Activities instead of sentences.

BBC World News – 6 players (3 players and 3 translators)

Rules

3 players speak in a made-up language.

As they are speaking, 3 translators will interpret for the audience in English.

Blocking

Speakers and translators need to pair up so that there are 3 pairs. Each pair should wear a ribbon or scarf of the same colour so that the audience can clearly see who the pairs are. Speakers should be on one side of the stage or space and the translators should be on the other side.

Script ideas

Three people are playing a game and one keeps cheating

A child tries to convince her parents that she is sick and needs to stay home from school

A talk show host is interviewing two people who have just lost 20 kilos each.

Hint

The players who are speaking in the made-up language need to be thinking in English so that their body language will help the translators.

Try it this way

Blindfold the translators so they cannot see the players' actions; they can only hear their words.

Translators can use only one word to translate what each player is saying.

Set alive – whole class

> ### *Rules*
> Choose an environment, e.g. a park.
>
> Spread out around the room.
>
> Find a place and become part of the suggested environment. You can be a tree, a park bench, a rubbish bin, etc. You can even be a sound effect.
>
> ### *Try it this way*
> Hold that environment until a new environment is suggested. Then everyone has to take on a new role.
>
> Suggested environments: a park, a school playground, a beach, a forest, a jungle, a zoo.

Numbers – 6 players

> ### *Rules*
> Each player is given a number from 1 to 10. Each sentence that the player speaks can contain only that number of words.
>
> ### *Hints*
> Players that only get one word will need to use a lot of body language.
>
> A person who has 3 words could say things like 'How are you?', 'I love you', 'No, no, no'.
>
> Players with more than 5 words will probably need to count their words on their fingers so that they don't lose count.
>
> ### *Try it this way*
> All players have the same number of words, but the audience can call out other numbers between 3 and 7.

Writing a monologue

Your purpose for writing a monologue is to engage your audience. Don't just present a list of things that have happened to the character or to convince your audience that a person you are describing is good, bad or stupid. These sorts of descriptions tend to make the audience yawn. They will lose interest and switch off.

There is nothing wrong with describing someone's past or personality, but make it interesting. Here are a few tips that will help you write a monologue. It is important that you always keep in mind why you are writing this monologue and who you are writing it for. There is nothing worse, for an audience, than to sit through a boring and uninteresting monologue.

1   WHO is speaking?

It is important to know what kind of person your character is.

Does he like reading super hero comics and nothing else?

Is she obsessed with wearing only things that are red?

Do they always need to have clean shoes?

You need to explain how your character would react in any situation. Your character's reactions should be different from your own reactions so that they will come across as an individual. Give your character an occupation and perhaps make a list of their favourite words. For example, your character may be a dentist's assistant who always checks her appearance in the mirror, including in the dentist's mirror.

2 WHY is the person speaking?

Always give your character a **reason** to be speaking. Think of speech as an action. Why is your character motivated to speak? In reality we speak only when something prompts us to. And we don't usually go on speaking unless we are telling a story, trying to calm someone down or trying to talk our way out of something.

Once you know who your character is, put them in a situation where they need to get something done. Make it a dramatic scene and it will keep your audience listening.

3 WHO is this person speaking TO?

Always stop to think who your audience is. Don't get too wrapped up in what you are writing and forget about the listener. Who is going to listen to this performer? What reaction is the message having on the listener?

Write your own monologues

These group activities will help you understand the process of how a monologue is constructed. They can be done in normal class time.

Empowering Your Pupils through Role-play © Rosanna Morales, Routledge 2008

Activity 1 – The story ball

You will need: a ball

This activity starts with a group standing in a circle. Someone should volunteer to start a simple story.

The person to start the story holds a ball. When they have finished speaking they throw the ball to another person in the circle, who then continues the story.

For example:

First person: When I was invited to my first school party I wore all the wrong things (*throws ball to the next person*).

Next person: I looked at myself in the mirror a hundred times before going out (*throws ball to the next person*).

Next person: I tried on nearly everything in my wardrobe (*throws ball to the next person*).

and so on . . .

Tips

Always talk in the first person (I think . . ., I was . . ., I went . . ., etc.)

Describe how you are feeling.

Describe the place you are in.

When you catch the ball you may not always want to speak, but keep the ball moving until someone is ready to continue with the story.

Empowering Your Pupils through Role-play © Rosanna Morales, Routledge 2008

Activity 2 – Sparkers

You will need: an observation journal

Write a monologue in your journal. Use any of the following 'sparkers' to start writing.

☐ Find an interesting newspaper article or heading and write the real story.

☐ Be a TV presenter reporting the news.

☐ Find a random word in the dictionary and use it as the first sentence of your monologue.

☐ Write the story behind an old photograph.

☐ Write about the memories of a particular toy.

☐ Write a stand-up routine about some funny observations of human behaviour.

☐ Write from an animal's point of view.

☐ Write from God's point of view.

☐ Write a telephone or chat line conversation.

☐ Write about a theme such as fear, guilt, pity, grief, anger, etc.

☐ Write about a specific time in the past or future.

Empowering Your Pupils through Role-play © Rosanna Morales, Routledge 2008

Activity 3 – What's going on?

You will need: an observation journal, photographs from newspapers or magazines

1   Collect photographs from magazines or newspapers and write your own set of questions to help you write your monologue.
2   Look at one of the images below to trigger the monologue. Write the monologue in your journal. You can use the questions listed or write your own to help you write your monologue.

Where is this taking place?
What did the clown do? What is he thinking?

What happens next?
How is this both funny and sad at the same time?

Write from the alien's or human's point of view.

What happens next?

What must it be like to be them?

What is each thinking at this moment?

What happens before or immediately after the photo is taken?

3   Pick a famous painting and put yourself inside the painting. What are you feeling? Where are you? How did you get there? What happens if you get out?

Activity 4 – Brainstorming

Choose a partner. Read each other's monologue out loud. Give each other some feedback, and brainstorm ways to improve the monologue. Then present your monologues to the class for evaluation. The more feedback you get the better your presentation will be.

Structuring an interactive play

An interactive play is one where the audience gets to choose what a character does at particular points in the story. In most plays we only get to see the writer's decision, so we don't know what might have happened if the character were given a different choice. Life is like that. Nearly every day we need to make important choices and we hardly ever get to find out what could have happened if we had said or done something different. Using interactive scripts, however, we can act out different scenarios as a rehearsal for real life. How many times have you said 'I should have said . . .' or 'I should have done . . .'?

In an interactive play you can set up the endings in as many ways as you wish.

Follow the simple flow chart below as a guide to writing an interactive play. You can add more endings if you wish. Use rectangles for the choices and diamonds for the outcomes.

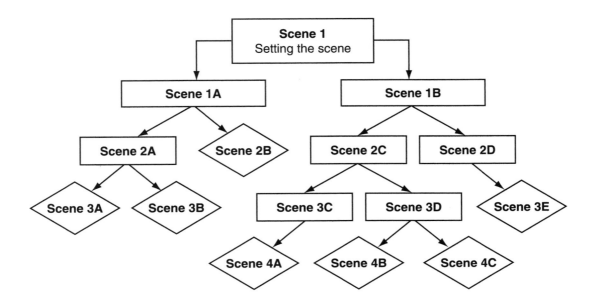

Empowering Your Pupils through Role-play © Rosanna Morales, Routledge 2008

Here are some suggestions that may help with writing the choice a character needs to make:

☐   Ignore or deal with a particular problem.

☐   Give up or keep going.

☐   Report an incident or not tell anyone.

☐   Accept an invitation or not.

Interviewing

One of the most important things to do when writing a play or monologue is research. You need to collect as many stories, articles and photographs as possible. Your research will help you describe a place, and the characters and their feelings.

You should write from other peoples' perspectives as well as from your own. A good way to create characters is to interview people. For example, if you wanted to write a monologue for a character who was lost in a desert for several days it could be difficult to write how that feels if you have not experienced it yourself. You may have an idea of what it feels to be scared and alone but you will probably not be able to describe it in as much detail as someone who has been in that situation.

Before interviewing someone, ask them in advance and give them plenty of time to prepare. Think about your questions. Practise your interview techniques on family and friends before approaching people you have not met before.

The following list will help you get organised:

☐   Write out your questions and give them to your interviewee beforehand.

☐   Take a writing pad and pen to the interview. Take good notes and record the date, time and place.

☐   If you are going to record the interview, ask permission first. Don't forget to take extra tapes and batteries.

☐   Always start with an easy question.

☐   Avoid questions that can be answered with just a *Yes* or *No.*

☐   Ask people about facts, description and their feelings.

☐   Don't do all the talking. Show interest and listen.

☐   Don't try to drag out answers. Some people find it hard to talk about certain things.

☐   When the interview is over thank the person for their time.